Change advisory board
Complete Self-Assessment Guide

The guidance in this Self-Assessment is based on Change advisory board best practices and standards in business process architecture, design and quality management. The guidance is also based on the professional judgment of the individual collaborators listed in the Acknowledgments.

Notice of rights

Trademarks

Table of Contents

About The Art of Service

The Art of Service, Business Process Architects since 2000, is dedicated to helping stakeholders achieve excellence.

Defining, designing, creating, and implementing a process to solve a stakeholders challenge or meet an objective is the most valuable role… In EVERY group, company, organization and department.

Unless you're talking a one-time, single-use project, there should be a process. Whether that process is managed and implemented by humans, AI, or a combination of the two, it needs to be designed by someone with a complex enough perspective to ask the right questions.

Someone capable of asking the right questions and step back and say, 'What are we really trying to accomplish here? And is there a different way to look at it?'

With The Art of Service's Standard Requirements Self-Assessments, we empower people who can do just that — whether their title is marketer, entrepreneur, manager, salesperson, consultant, Business Process Manager, executive assistant, IT Manager, CIO etc... —they are the people who rule the future. They are people who watch the process as it happens, and ask the right questions to make the process work better.

Contact us when you need any support with this Self-Assessment and any help with templates, blue-prints and examples of standard documents you might need:

http://theartofservice.com
service@theartofservice.com

Acknowledgments

This checklist was developed under the auspices of The Art of Service, chaired by Gerardus Blokdyk.

Representatives from several client companies participated in the preparation of this Self-Assessment.

Our deepest gratitude goes out to Matt Champagne, Ph.D. Surveys Expert, for his invaluable help and advise in structuring the Self Assessment.

Mr Champagne can be contacted at http://matthewchampagne.com/

In addition, we are thankful for the design and printing services provided.

Included Resources - how to access

Included with your purchase of the book is the Change advisory board Self-Assessment Spreadsheet Dashboard which contains all questions and Self-Assessment areas and auto-generates insights, graphs, and project RACI planning - all with examples to get you started right away.

Get it now- you will be glad you did - do it now, before you forget.

How? Simply send an email to **access@theartofservice.com** with this books' title in the subject to get the Change advisory board Self Assessment Tool right away.

Your feedback is invaluable to us

If you recently bought this book, we would love to hear from you! You can do this by writing a review on amazon (or the online store where you purchased this book) about your last purchase! As part of our continual service improvement process, we love to hear real client experiences and feedback.

How does it work?
To post a review on Amazon, just log in to your account and click on the Create Your Own Review button (under Customer Reviews) of the relevant product page. You can find examples of product reviews in Amazon. If you purchased from another online store, simply follow their procedures.

What happens when I submit my review?
Once you have submitted your review, send us an email at review@theartofservice.com with the link to your review so we can properly thank you for your feedback.

Purpose of this Self-Assessment

This Self-Assessment has been developed to improve understanding of the requirements and elements of Change advisory board, based on best practices and standards in business process architecture, design and quality management.

It is designed to allow for a rapid Self-Assessment to determine how closely existing management practices and procedures correspond to the elements of the Self-Assessment.

The criteria of requirements and elements of Change advisory board have been rephrased in the format of a Self-Assessment questionnaire, with a seven-criterion scoring system, as explained in this document.

In this format, even with limited background knowledge of Change advisory board, a manager can quickly review existing operations to determine how they measure up to the standards. This in turn can serve as the starting point of a 'gap analysis' to identify management tools or system elements that might usefully be implemented in the organization to help improve overall performance.

How to use the Self-Assessment

On the following pages are a series of questions to identify to what extent your Change advisory board initiative is complete in comparison to the requirements set in standards.

To facilitate answering the questions, there is a space in front of each question to enter a score on a scale of '1' to '5'.

1 Strongly Disagree

2 Disagree

3 Neutral

4 Agree

5 Strongly Agree

Read the question and rate it with the following in front of mind:

**'In my belief,
the answer to this question is clearly defined'.**

There are two ways in which you can choose to interpret this statement;
1. how aware are you that the answer to the question is clearly defined
2. for more in-depth analysis you can choose to gather evidence and confirm the answer to the question. This

obviously will take more time, most Self-Assessment users opt for the first way to interpret the question and dig deeper later on based on the outcome of the overall Self-Assessment.

A score of '1' would mean that the answer is not clear at all, where a '5' would mean the answer is crystal clear and defined. Leave emtpy when the question is not applicable or you don't want to answer it, you can skip it without affecting your score. Write your score in the space provided.

After you have responded to all the appropriate statements in each section, compute your average score for that section, using the formula provided, and round to the nearest tenth. Then transfer to the corresponding spoke in the Change advisory board Scorecard on the second next page of the Self-Assessment.

Your completed Change advisory board Scorecard will give you a clear presentation of which Change advisory board areas need attention.

Change advisory board Scorecard Example

Example of how the finalized Scorecard can look like:

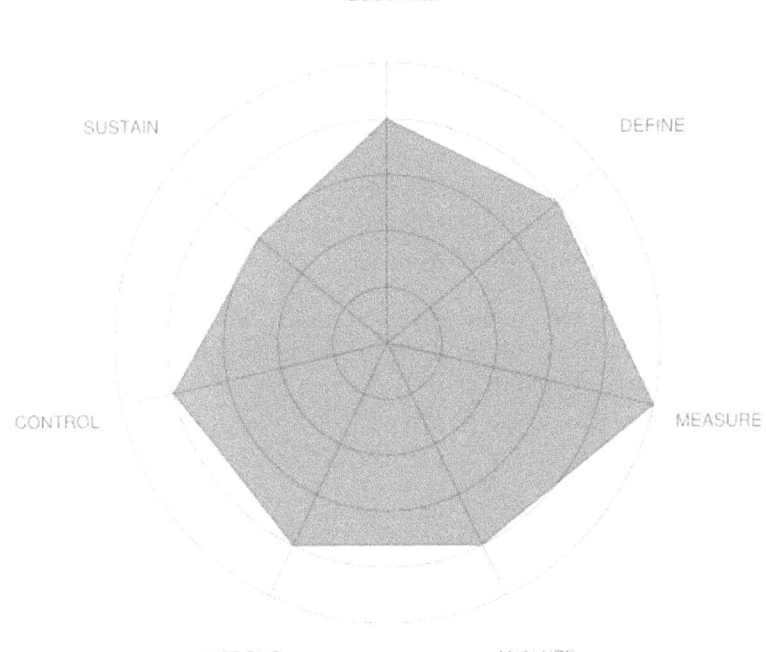

Change advisory board Scorecard

Your Scores:

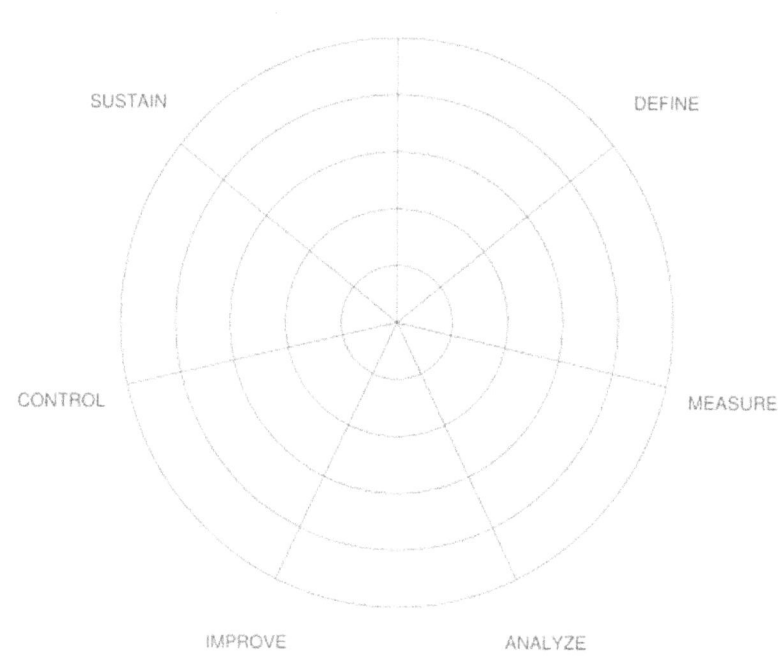

BEGINNING OF THE SELF-ASSESSMENT:

CRITERION #1: RECOGNIZE

INTENT: Be aware of the need for change. Recognize that there is an unfavorable variation, problem or symptom.

In my belief, the answer to this question is clearly defined:

5 Strongly Agree

4 Agree

3 Neutral

2 Disagree

1 Strongly Disagree

1. Who needs to know about Change advisory board ?
<--- Score

2. Can Management personnel recognize the monetary benefit of Change advisory board?
<--- Score

3. Who else hopes to benefit from it?

<--- Score

4. Are there recognized Change advisory board problems?
<--- Score

5. Does Change advisory board create potential expectations in other areas that need to be recognized and considered?
<--- Score

6. How do you identify the kinds of information that you will need?
<--- Score

7. What information do users need?
<--- Score

8. What do we need to start doing?
<--- Score

9. What should be considered when identifying available resources, constraints, and deadlines?
<--- Score

10. Does our organization need more Change advisory board education?
<--- Score

11. How do we Identify specific Change advisory board investment and emerging trends?
<--- Score

12. Are controls defined to recognize and contain problems?
<--- Score

13. What does Change advisory board success mean to the stakeholders?
<--- Score

14. What is the smallest subset of the problem we can usefully solve?
<--- Score

15. What is the smallest subset of the problem we can usefully solve?
<--- Score

16. Will new equipment/products be required to facilitate Change advisory board delivery for example is new software needed?
<--- Score

17. What vendors make products that address the Change advisory board needs?
<--- Score

18. Think about the people you identified for your Change advisory board project and the project responsibilities you would assign to them. what kind of training do you think they would need to perform these responsibilities effectively?
<--- Score

19. Will it solve real problems?
<--- Score

20. Are there Change advisory board problems defined?
<--- Score

21. For your Change advisory board project, identify and describe the business environment. is there more than one layer to the business environment?

<--- Score

22. As a sponsor, customer or management, how important is it to meet goals, objectives?

<--- Score

23. What else needs to be measured?

<--- Score

24. Are there any specific expectations or concerns about the Change advisory board team, Change advisory board itself?

<--- Score

25. What tools and technologies are needed for a custom Change advisory board project?

<--- Score

26. Will Change advisory board deliverables need to be tested and, if so, by whom?

<--- Score

27. What are the expected benefits of Change advisory board to the business?

<--- Score

28. Why do we need to keep records?

<--- Score

29. How do you identify the information basis for later specification of performance or acceptance criteria?

<--- Score

30. What are the business objectives to be achieved with Change advisory board?
<--- Score

31. What would happen if Change advisory board weren't done?
<--- Score

32. Consider your own Change advisory board project. what types of organizational problems do you think might be causing or affecting your problem, based on the work done so far?
<--- Score

33. Is it clear when you think of the day ahead of you what activities and tasks you need to complete?
<--- Score

34. What training and capacity building actions are needed to implement proposed reforms?
<--- Score

35. Who defines the rules in relation to any given issue?
<--- Score

36. What problems are you facing and how do you consider Change advisory board will circumvent those obstacles?
<--- Score

37. How does it fit into our organizational needs and tasks?

<--- Score

38. How are we going to measure success?
<--- Score

39. What prevents me from making the changes I know will make me a more effective Change advisory board leader?
<--- Score

40. How are the Change advisory board's objectives aligned to the organization's overall business strategy?
<--- Score

41. Have you identified your Change advisory board key performance indicators?
<--- Score

42. Who had the original idea?
<--- Score

43. What situation(s) led to this Change advisory board Self Assessment?
<--- Score

44. Do we know what we need to know about this topic?
<--- Score

45. How do you prevent errors and rework?
<--- Score

46. When a Change advisory board manager recognizes a problem, what options are available?
<--- Score

47. How do you assess your Change advisory board workforce capability and capacity needs, including skills, competencies, and staffing levels?
<--- Score

48. How can auditing be a preventative security measure?
<--- Score

49. How much are sponsors, customers, partners, stakeholders involved in Change advisory board? In other words, what are the risks, if Change advisory board does not deliver successfully?
<--- Score

50. Will a response program recognize when a crisis occurs and provide some level of response?
<--- Score

Add up total points for this section:
_ _ _ _ _ = Total points for this section

Divided by: _ _ _ _ _ _ (number of statements answered) = _ _ _ _ _ _
Average score for this section

Transfer your score to the Change advisory board Index at the beginning of the Self-Assessment.

CRITERION #2: DEFINE:

INTENT: Formulate the business problem. Define the problem, needs and objectives.

In my belief, the answer to this question is clearly defined:

5 Strongly Agree

4 Agree

3 Neutral

2 Disagree

1 Strongly Disagree

1. What critical content must be communicated – who, what, when, where, and how?
<--- Score

2. Who are the Change advisory board improvement team members, including Management Leads and Coaches?
<--- Score

3. Has/have the customer(s) been identified?
<--- Score

4. Is the improvement team aware of the different versions of a process: what they think it is vs. what it actually is vs. what it should be vs. what it could be?
<--- Score

5. Has anyone else (internal or external to the organization) attempted to solve this problem or a similar one before? If so, what knowledge can be leveraged from these previous efforts?
<--- Score

6. Is Change advisory board currently on schedule according to the plan?
<--- Score

7. What are the Roles and Responsibilities for each team member and its leadership? Where is this documented?
<--- Score

8. Has a project plan, Gantt chart, or similar been developed/completed?
<--- Score

9. How was the 'as is' process map developed, reviewed, verified and validated?
<--- Score

10. Are business processes mapped?
<--- Score

11. How do senior leaders promote an environment that fosters and requires legal and

ethical behavior?
<--- Score

12. Is the scope of Change advisory board defined?
<--- Score

13. Is the current 'as is' process being followed? If not, what are the discrepancies?
<--- Score

14. Has the direction changed at all during the course of Change advisory board? If so, when did it change and why?
<--- Score

15. Has the Change advisory board work been fairly and/or equitably divided and delegated among team members who are qualified and capable to perform the work? Has everyone contributed?
<--- Score

16. Are approval levels defined for contracts and supplements to contracts?
<--- Score

17. What baselines are required to be defined and managed?
<--- Score

18. Have all basic functions of Change advisory board been defined?
<--- Score

19. When are meeting minutes sent out? Who is on the distribution list?
<--- Score

20. When is the estimated completion date?
<--- Score

21. Do the problem and goal statements meet the SMART criteria (specific, measurable, attainable, relevant, and time-bound)?
<--- Score

22. Have the customer needs been translated into specific, measurable requirements? How?
<--- Score

23. Does the team have regular meetings?
<--- Score

24. What defines Best in Class?
<--- Score

25. Are improvement team members fully trained on Change advisory board?
<--- Score

26. Is a fully trained team formed, supported, and committed to work on the Change advisory board improvements?
<--- Score

27. Has the improvement team collected the 'voice of the customer' (obtained feedback – qualitative and quantitative)?
<--- Score

28. Is there regularly 100% attendance at the team meetings? If not, have appointed substitutes attended to preserve cross-functionality and full

representation?
<--- Score

29. How would one define Change advisory board leadership?
<--- Score

30. What are the rough order estimates on cost savings/opportunities that Change advisory board brings?
<--- Score

31. Who defines (or who defined) the rules and roles?
<--- Score

32. When was the Change advisory board start date?
<--- Score

33. How would you define the culture here?
<--- Score

34. Do we all define Change advisory board in the same way?
<--- Score

35. Is Change advisory board linked to key business goals and objectives?
<--- Score

36. What key business process output measure(s) does Change advisory board leverage and how?
<--- Score

37. What organizational structure is required?
<--- Score

38. Is the team adequately staffed with the desired cross-functionality? If not, what additional resources are available to the team?
<--- Score

39. Are roles and responsibilities formally defined?
<--- Score

40. What constraints exist that might impact the team?
<--- Score

41. How can the value of Change advisory board be defined?
<--- Score

42. How do you keep key subject matter experts in the loop?
<--- Score

43. Is there a Change advisory board management charter, including business case, problem and goal statements, scope, milestones, roles and responsibilities, communication plan?
<--- Score

44. Are there different segments of customers?
<--- Score

45. What are the compelling business reasons for embarking on Change advisory board?
<--- Score

46. Are security/privacy roles and responsibilities formally defined?
<--- Score

47. Is there a critical path to deliver Change advisory board results?

<--- Score

48. What customer feedback methods were used to solicit their input?

<--- Score

49. Is the team sponsored by a champion or business leader?

<--- Score

50. Are customer(s) identified and segmented according to their different needs and requirements?

<--- Score

51. What are the dynamics of the communication plan?

<--- Score

52. What specifically is the problem? Where does it occur? When does it occur? What is its extent?

<--- Score

53. Are there any constraints known that bear on the ability to perform Change advisory board work? How is the team addressing them?

<--- Score

54. Has a high-level 'as is' process map been completed, verified and validated?

<--- Score

55. Is full participation by members in regularly held team meetings guaranteed?

<--- Score

56. In what way can we redefine the criteria of choice in our category in our favor, as Method introduced style and design to cleaning and Virgin America returned glamor to flying?
<--- Score

57. Have specific policy objectives been defined?
<--- Score

58. How does the Change advisory board manager ensure against scope creep?
<--- Score

59. Will team members regularly document their Change advisory board work?
<--- Score

60. What would be the goal or target for a Change advisory board's improvement team?
<--- Score

61. Is there a completed SIPOC representation, describing the Suppliers, Inputs, Process, Outputs, and Customers?
<--- Score

62. Are audit criteria, scope, frequency and methods defined?
<--- Score

63. Has everyone on the team, including the team leaders, been properly trained?
<--- Score

64. Is the team formed and are team leaders (Coaches and Management Leads) assigned?
<--- Score

65. Will team members perform Change advisory board work when assigned and in a timely fashion?
<--- Score

66. How is the team tracking and documenting its work?
<--- Score

67. How did the Change advisory board manager receive input to the development of a Change advisory board improvement plan and the estimated completion dates/times of each activity?
<--- Score

68. Are customers identified and high impact areas defined?
<--- Score

69. Are accountability and ownership for Change advisory board clearly defined?
<--- Score

70. If substitutes have been appointed, have they been briefed on the Change advisory board goals and received regular communications as to the progress to date?
<--- Score

71. Is the team equipped with available and reliable resources?
<--- Score

72. Is there a completed, verified, and validated high-level 'as is' (not 'should be' or 'could be') business process map?
<--- Score

73. How will variation in the actual durations of each activity be dealt with to ensure that the expected Change advisory board results are met?
<--- Score

74. How often are the team meetings?
<--- Score

75. Are team charters developed?
<--- Score

76. Has a team charter been developed and communicated?
<--- Score

77. Have all of the relationships been defined properly?
<--- Score

78. Are Required Metrics Defined?
<--- Score

79. Are task requirements clearly defined?
<--- Score

80. How and when will the baselines be defined?
<--- Score

81. Are different versions of process maps needed to account for the different types of inputs?
<--- Score

82. How will the Change advisory board team and the organization measure complete success of Change advisory board?
<--- Score

83. Is Change advisory board Required?
<--- Score

84. What is the minimum educational requirement for potential new hires?
<--- Score

85. Is the Change advisory board scope manageable?
<--- Score

86. What tools and roadmaps did you use for getting through the Define phase?
<--- Score

87. Is data collected and displayed to better understand customer(s) critical needs and requirements.
<--- Score

88. Is it clearly defined in and to your organization what you do?
<--- Score

89. What are the boundaries of the scope? What is in bounds and what is not? What is the start point? What is the stop point?
<--- Score

90. In what way can we redefine the criteria of choice clients have in our category in our favor?

<--- Score

Add up total points for this section:
_____ = Total points for this section

Divided by: _____ (number of
statements answered) = _____
Average score for this section

Transfer your score to the Change
advisory board Index at the beginning
of the Self-Assessment.

CRITERION #3: MEASURE:

INTENT: Gather the correct data.
Measure the current performance and
evolution of the situation.

In my belief, the answer to this
question is clearly defined:

5 Strongly Agree

4 Agree

3 Neutral

2 Disagree

1 Strongly Disagree

1. What should be measured?
<--- Score

2. What about Change advisory board Analysis of results?
<--- Score

3. Does the practice systematically track and analyze outcomes related for accountability and quality

improvement?

<--- Score

4. Which customers cant participate in our Change advisory board domain because they lack skills, wealth, or convenient access to existing solutions?

<--- Score

5. What are the costs of reform?

<--- Score

6. What are our key indicators that you will measure, analyze and track?

<--- Score

7. Are there any easy-to-implement alternatives to Change advisory board? Sometimes other solutions are available that do not require the cost implications of a full-blown project?

<--- Score

8. Will We Aggregate Measures across Priorities?

<--- Score

9. What data was collected (past, present, future/ ongoing)?

<--- Score

10. Are priorities and opportunities deployed to your suppliers, partners, and collaborators to ensure organizational alignment?

<--- Score

11. How large is the gap between current performance and the customer-specified (goal) performance?

<--- Score

12. Are there measurements based on task performance?
<--- Score

13. Why do the measurements/indicators matter?
<--- Score

14. Is key measure data collection planned and executed, process variation displayed and communicated and performance baselined?
<--- Score

15. What is the total cost related to deploying Change advisory board, including any consulting or professional services?
<--- Score

16. How can we measure the performance?
<--- Score

17. What are the uncertainties surrounding estimates of impact?
<--- Score

18. How will your organization measure success?
<--- Score

19. How to measure lifecycle phases?
<--- Score

20. How is Knowledge Management Measured?
<--- Score

21. Who participated in the data collection for

measurements?
<--- Score

22. How are measurements made?
<--- Score

23. What evidence is there and what is measured?
<--- Score

24. Have the types of risks that may impact Change advisory board been identified and analyzed?
<--- Score

25. Was a data collection plan established?
<--- Score

26. How do we focus on what is right -not who is right?
<--- Score

27. What are measures?
<--- Score

28. What is measured?
<--- Score

29. Do we effectively measure and reward individual and team performance?
<--- Score

30. How frequently do we track measures?
<--- Score

31. How will success or failure be measured?
<--- Score

32. What are my customers expectations and measures?
<--- Score

33. Can We Measure the Return on Analysis?
<--- Score

34. What charts has the team used to display the components of variation in the process?
<--- Score

35. What measurements are being captured?
<--- Score

36. Is data collection planned and executed?
<--- Score

37. Can we do Change advisory board without complex (expensive) analysis?
<--- Score

38. What is an unallowable cost?
<--- Score

39. Is data collected on key measures that were identified?
<--- Score

40. Which customers can't participate in our market because they lack skills, wealth, or convenient access to existing solutions?
<--- Score

41. How is the value delivered by Change advisory board being measured?
<--- Score

42. Is Process Variation Displayed/Communicated?
<--- Score

43. What is the right balance of time and resources between investigation, analysis, and discussion and dissemination?
<--- Score

44. Why Measure?
<--- Score

45. How are you going to measure success?
<--- Score

46. How do you identify and analyze stakeholders and their interests?
<--- Score

47. What has the team done to assure the stability and accuracy of the measurement process?
<--- Score

48. Do staff have the necessary skills to collect, analyze, and report data?
<--- Score

49. Do we aggressively reward and promote the people who have the biggest impact on creating excellent Change advisory board services/ products?
<--- Score

50. How do you measure success?
<--- Score

51. How is progress measured?
<--- Score

52. What will be measured?
<--- Score

53. How to measure variability?
<--- Score

54. Why do measure/indicators matter?
<--- Score

55. How will effects be measured?
<--- Score

56. Who should receive measurement reports ?
<--- Score

57. Meeting the challenge: are missed Change advisory board opportunities costing us money?
<--- Score

58. Does Change advisory board analysis isolate the fundamental causes of problems?
<--- Score

59. What to measure and why?
<--- Score

60. What key measures identified indicate the performance of the business process?
<--- Score

61. Among the Change advisory board product and service cost to be estimated, which is considered hardest to estimate?

<--- Score

62. What particular quality tools did the team find helpful in establishing measurements?
<--- Score

63. Are key measures identified and agreed upon?
<--- Score

64. Does Change advisory board systematically track and analyze outcomes for accountability and quality improvement?
<--- Score

65. Are you taking your company in the direction of better and revenue or cheaper and cost?
<--- Score

66. Which methods and measures do you use to determine workforce engagement and workforce satisfaction?
<--- Score

67. Have changes been properly/adequately analyzed for effect?
<--- Score

68. Why identify and analyze stakeholders and their interests?
<--- Score

69. Where is it measured?
<--- Score

70. What methods are feasible and acceptable to estimate the impact of reforms?

<--- Score

71. Which Stakeholder Characteristics Are Analyzed?
<--- Score

72. Is this an issue for analysis or intuition?
<--- Score

73. Is there a Performance Baseline?
<--- Score

74. How can you measure Change advisory board in a systematic way?
<--- Score

75. What are the agreed upon definitions of the high impact areas, defect(s), unit(s), and opportunities that will figure into the process capability metrics?
<--- Score

76. What potential environmental factors impact the Change advisory board effort?
<--- Score

77. How will you measure your Change advisory board effectiveness?
<--- Score

78. Is the solution cost-effective?
<--- Score

79. How will measures be used to manage and adapt?
<--- Score

80. Are we taking our company in the direction of better and revenue or cheaper and cost?

<--- Score

81. What are your key Change advisory board organizational performance measures, including key short and longer-term financial measures?
<--- Score

82. What measurements are possible, practicable and meaningful?
<--- Score

83. Are the units of measure consistent?
<--- Score

84. What are the types and number of measures to use?
<--- Score

85. How frequently do you track Change advisory board measures?
<--- Score

86. Does Change advisory board analysis show the relationships among important Change advisory board factors?
<--- Score

87. Are the measurements objective?
<--- Score

88. Are high impact defects defined and identified in the business process?
<--- Score

89. Have you found any 'ground fruit' or 'low-hanging fruit' for immediate remedies to the gap in

performance?
<--- Score

90. Why should we expend time and effort to implement measurement?
<--- Score

91. How Will We Measure Success?
<--- Score

92. Is a solid data collection plan established that includes measurement systems analysis?
<--- Score

93. Are losses documented, analyzed, and remedial processes developed to prevent future losses?
<--- Score

94. How do we do risk analysis of rare, cascading, catastrophic events?
<--- Score

95. What Relevant Entities could be measured?
<--- Score

96. Are process variation components displayed/ communicated using suitable charts, graphs, plots?
<--- Score

97. Have the concerns of stakeholders to help identify and define potential barriers been obtained and analyzed?
<--- Score

98. When is Knowledge Management Measured?
<--- Score

99. Is performance measured?
<--- Score

100. Customer Measures: How Do Customers See Us?
<--- Score

101. What are the key input variables? What are the key process variables? What are the key output variables?
<--- Score

102. Does the Change advisory board task fit the client's priorities?
<--- Score

103. Have all non-recommended alternatives been analyzed in sufficient detail?
<--- Score

104. Is long term and short term variability accounted for?
<--- Score

105. How do senior leaders create a focus on action to accomplish the organization s objectives and improve performance?
<--- Score

106. Is it possible to estimate the impact of unanticipated complexity such as wrong or failed assumptions, feedback, etc. on proposed reforms?
<--- Score

Add up total points for this section:
_ _ _ _ _ = Total points for this section

Divided by: _ _ _ _ _ _   (number of
statements answered) = _ _ _ _ _ _
Average score for this section

Transfer your score to the Change
advisory board Index at the beginning
of the Self-Assessment.

CRITERION #4: ANALYZE:

INTENT: Analyze causes, assumptions and hypotheses.

In my belief, the answer to this question is clearly defined:

5 Strongly Agree

4 Agree

3 Neutral

2 Disagree

1 Strongly Disagree

1. What conclusions were drawn from the team's data collection and analysis? How did the team reach these conclusions?
<--- Score

2. Do our leaders quickly bounce back from setbacks?
<--- Score

3. What are your current levels and trends in

key measures or indicators of Change advisory board product and process performance that are important to and directly serve your customers? how do these results compare with the performance of your competitors and other organizations with similar offerings?

<--- Score

4. When conducting a business process reengineering study, what should we look for when trying to identify business processes to change?

<--- Score

5. What process should we select for improvement?

<--- Score

6. What are the best opportunities for value improvement?

<--- Score

7. How do you use Change advisory board data and information to support organizational decision making and innovation?

<--- Score

8. What did the team gain from developing a sub-process map?

<--- Score

9. What are the revised rough estimates of the financial savings/opportunity for Change advisory board improvements?

<--- Score

10. Are gaps between current performance and the

goal performance identified?
<--- Score

11. A compounding model resolution with available relevant data can often provide insight towards a solution methodology; which Change advisory board models, tools and techniques are necessary?
<--- Score

12. Identify an operational issue in your organization. for example, could a particular task be done more quickly or more efficiently?
<--- Score

13. How do you measure the Operational performance of your key work systems and processes, including productivity, cycle time, and other appropriate measures of process effectiveness, efficiency, and innovation?
<--- Score

14. Did any additional data need to be collected?
<--- Score

15. Can we add value to the current Change advisory board decision-making process (largely qualitative) by incorporating uncertainty modeling (more quantitative)?
<--- Score

16. Think about some of the processes you undertake within your organization. which do you own?
<--- Score

17. An organizationally feasible system request is one that considers the mission, goals and objectives of the organization. key questions are: is the solution request practical and will it solve a problem or take advantage of an opportunity to achieve company goals?
<--- Score

18. Do you, as a leader, bounce back quickly from setbacks?
<--- Score

19. How do we promote understanding that opportunity for improvement is not criticism of the status quo, or the people who created the status quo?
<--- Score

20. Did any value-added analysis or 'lean thinking' take place to identify some of the gaps shown on the 'as is' process map?
<--- Score

21. Were any designed experiments used to generate additional insight into the data analysis?
<--- Score

22. Where is the data coming from to measure compliance?
<--- Score

23. Is Data and process analysis, root cause analysis and quantifying the gap/opportunity in place?
<--- Score

24. What controls do we have in place to protect data?

<--- Score

25. Is the gap/opportunity displayed and communicated in financial terms?
<--- Score

26. How is the way you as the leader think and process information affecting your organizational culture?
<--- Score

27. What is the cost of poor quality as supported by the team's analysis?
<--- Score

28. What other organizational variables, such as reward systems or communication systems, affect the performance of this Change advisory board process?
<--- Score

29. What are the disruptive Change advisory board technologies that enable our organization to radically change our business processes?
<--- Score

30. What quality tools were used to get through the analyze phase?
<--- Score

31. Think about the functions involved in your Change advisory board project. what processes flow from these functions?
<--- Score

32. What other jobs or tasks affect the performance of the steps in the Change advisory

board process?
<--- Score

33. What were the crucial 'moments of truth' on the process map?
<--- Score

34. What tools were used to narrow the list of possible causes?
<--- Score

35. What tools were used to generate the list of possible causes?
<--- Score

36. Is the performance gap determined?
<--- Score

37. What are your current levels and trends in key Change advisory board measures or indicators of product and process performance that are important to and directly serve your customers?
<--- Score

38. How does the organization define, manage, and improve its Change advisory board processes?
<--- Score

39. How do mission and objectives affect the Change advisory board processes of our organization?
<--- Score

40. How was the detailed process map generated, verified, and validated?
<--- Score

41. What were the financial benefits resulting from any 'ground fruit or low-hanging fruit' (quick fixes)?
<--- Score

42. Was a cause-and-effect diagram used to explore the different types of causes (or sources of variation)?
<--- Score

43. How often will data be collected for measures?
<--- Score

44. What are our Change advisory board Processes?
<--- Score

45. Have any additional benefits been identified that will result from closing all or most of the gaps?
<--- Score

46. Was a detailed process map created to amplify critical steps of the 'as is' business process?
<--- Score

47. Is the Change advisory board process severely broken such that a re-design is necessary?
<--- Score

48. Record-keeping requirements flow from the records needed as inputs, outputs, controls and for transformation of a Change advisory board process. ask yourself: are the records needed as inputs to the Change advisory board process available?
<--- Score

49. What successful thing are we doing today that

may be blinding us to new growth opportunities?
<--- Score

50. Were there any improvement opportunities identified from the process analysis?
<--- Score

51. Were Pareto charts (or similar) used to portray the 'heavy hitters' (or key sources of variation)?
<--- Score

52. Have the problem and goal statements been updated to reflect the additional knowledge gained from the analyze phase?
<--- Score

53. What does the data say about the performance of the business process?
<--- Score

54. Do your employees have the opportunity to do what they do best everyday?
<--- Score

55. Is the suppliers process defined and controlled?
<--- Score

56. Is the suppliers process defined and controlled?
<--- Score

Add up total points for this section:
_ _ _ _ _ = Total points for this section

Divided by: _ _ _ _ _ _ (number of statements answered) = _ _ _ _ _ _

Average score for this section

Transfer your score to the Change
advisory board Index at the beginning
of the Self-Assessment.

CRITERION #5: IMPROVE:

INTENT: Develop a practical solution. Innovate, establish and test the solution and to measure the results.

In my belief, the answer to this question is clearly defined:

5 Strongly Agree

4 Agree

3 Neutral

2 Disagree

1 Strongly Disagree

1. What are the implications of this decision 10 minutes, 10 months, and 10 years from now?
<--- Score

2. Is a contingency plan established?
<--- Score

3. Were any criteria developed to assist the team in testing and evaluating potential solutions?

<--- Score

4. How can skill-level changes improve Change advisory board?
<--- Score

5. What is the team's contingency plan for potential problems occurring in implementation?
<--- Score

6. What tools were most useful during the improve phase?
<--- Score

7. How do you improve workforce health, safety, and security? What are your performance measures and improvement goals for each of these workforce needs and what are any significant differences in these factors and performance measures or targets for different workplace environments?
<--- Score

8. How will the team or the process owner(s) monitor the implementation plan to see that it is working as intended?
<--- Score

9. How do you improve your likelihood of success ?
<--- Score

10. How do the Change advisory board results compare with the performance of your competitors and other organizations with similar offerings?
<--- Score

11. Are there any constraints (technical, political, cultural, or otherwise) that would inhibit certain solutions?
<--- Score

12. Does the goal represent a desired result that can be measured?
<--- Score

13. Are we Assessing Change advisory board and Risk?
<--- Score

14. How can we improve performance?
<--- Score

15. What is the risk?
<--- Score

16. Was a pilot designed for the proposed solution(s)?
<--- Score

17. Is the measure understandable to a variety of people?
<--- Score

18. What improvements have been achieved?
<--- Score

19. How will the organization know that the solution worked?
<--- Score

20. What tools were used to evaluate the potential solutions?
<--- Score

21. How does the team improve its work?
<--- Score

22. How significant is the improvement in the eyes of the end user?
<--- Score

23. Who will be using the results of the measurement activities?
<--- Score

24. How do we measure risk?
<--- Score

25. How do we improve productivity?
<--- Score

26. What attendant changes will need to be made to ensure that the solution is successful?
<--- Score

27. Who controls key decisions that will be made?
<--- Score

28. What went well, what should change, what can improve?
<--- Score

29. What communications are necessary to support the implementation of the solution?
<--- Score

30. How did the team generate the list of possible solutions?
<--- Score

31. Are possible solutions generated and tested?
<--- Score

32. For decision problems, how do you develop a decision statement?
<--- Score

33. How does the solution remove the key sources of issues discovered in the analyze phase?
<--- Score

34. Risk events: what are the things that could go wrong?
<--- Score

35. How do we go about Comparing Change advisory board approaches/solutions?
<--- Score

36. What tools were used to tap into the creativity and encourage 'outside the box' thinking?
<--- Score

37. Is the optimal solution selected based on testing and analysis?
<--- Score

38. Is Supporting Change advisory board documentation required?
<--- Score

39. For estimation problems, how do you develop an estimation statement?
<--- Score

40. Risk factors: what are the characteristics of Change advisory board that make it risky?
<--- Score

41. Is the implementation plan designed?
<--- Score

42. Is there a high likelihood that any recommendations will achieve their intended results?
<--- Score

43. What can we do to improve?
<--- Score

44. Is the solution technically practical?
<--- Score

45. How do we measure improved Change advisory board service perception, and satisfaction?
<--- Score

46. What needs improvement?
<--- Score

47. What actually has to improve and by how much?
<--- Score

48. What lessons, if any, from a pilot were incorporated into the design of the full-scale solution?
<--- Score

49. How will you measure the results?
<--- Score

50. How to Improve?
<--- Score

51. In the past few months, what is the smallest change we have made that has had the biggest positive result? What was it about that small change that produced the large return?
<--- Score

52. Do we cover the five essential competencies-Communication, Collaboration,Innovation, Adaptability, and Leadership that improve an organization's ability to leverage the new Change advisory board in a volatile global economy?
<--- Score

53. Why improve in the first place?
<--- Score

54. How do we Improve Change advisory board service perception, and satisfaction?
<--- Score

55. Is a solution implementation plan established, including schedule/work breakdown structure, resources, risk management plan, cost/budget, and control plan?
<--- Score

56. Is there a small-scale pilot for proposed improvement(s)? What conclusions were drawn from the outcomes of a pilot?
<--- Score

57. How can we improve Change advisory board?

<--- Score

58. What do we want to improve?
<--- Score

59. Who will be responsible for making the decisions to include or exclude requested changes once Change advisory board is underway?
<--- Score

60. What resources are required for the improvement effort?
<--- Score

61. Is pilot data collected and analyzed?
<--- Score

62. How will you know when its improved?
<--- Score

63. What is the magnitude of the improvements?
<--- Score

64. If you could go back in time five years, what decision would you make differently? What is your best guess as to what decision you're making today you might regret five years from now?
<--- Score

65. Are the best solutions selected?
<--- Score

66. To what extent does management recognize Change advisory board as a tool to increase the results?
<--- Score

67. What should a proof of concept or pilot accomplish?

<--- Score

68. Describe the design of the pilot and what tests were conducted, if any?

<--- Score

69. What to do with the results or outcomes of measurements?

<--- Score

70. How do we decide how much to remunerate an employee?

<--- Score

71. How do we keep improving Change advisory board?

<--- Score

72. Do we get business results?

<--- Score

73. How Do We Link Measurement and Risk?

<--- Score

74. What does the 'should be' process map/design look like?

<--- Score

75. How do you measure progress and evaluate training effectiveness?

<--- Score

76. How do you use other indicators, such as

workforce retention, absenteeism, grievances, safety, and productivity, to assess and improve workforce engagement?
<--- Score

77. How important is the completion of a recognized college or graduate-level degree program in the hiring decision?
<--- Score

78. Are new and improved process ('should be') maps developed?
<--- Score

79. Is there a cost/benefit analysis of optimal solution(s)?
<--- Score

80. Who are the people involved in developing and implementing Change advisory board?
<--- Score

81. How will you know that you have improved?
<--- Score

82. What error proofing will be done to address some of the discrepancies observed in the 'as is' process?
<--- Score

83. Who will be responsible for documenting the Change advisory board requirements in detail?
<--- Score

84. What evaluation strategy is needed and what needs to be done to assure its implementation and use?

<--- Score

85. What is the implementation plan?
<--- Score

86. Are improved process ('should be') maps modified based on pilot data and analysis?
<--- Score

87. Can the solution be designed and implemented within an acceptable time period?
<--- Score

88. At what point will vulnerability assessments be performed once Change advisory board is put into production (e.g., ongoing Risk Management after implementation)?
<--- Score

89. What is Change advisory board's impact on utilizing the best solution(s)?
<--- Score

90. Who controls the risk?
<--- Score

91. How will we know that a change is improvement?
<--- Score

92. What were the underlying assumptions on the cost-benefit analysis?
<--- Score

Add up total points for this section:
_ _ _ _ _ = Total points for this section

Divided by: _____ (number of
statements answered) = _____
Average score for this section

Transfer your score to the Change
advisory board Index at the beginning
of the Self-Assessment.

CRITERION #6: CONTROL:

INTENT: Implement the practical solution. Maintain the performance and correct possible complications.

In my belief, the answer to this question is clearly defined:

5 Strongly Agree

4 Agree

3 Neutral

2 Disagree

1 Strongly Disagree

1. Where do ideas that reach policy makers and planners as proposals for Change advisory board strengthening and reform actually originate?
<--- Score

2. How do controls support value?
<--- Score

3. Does the response plan contain a definite closed

loop continual improvement scheme (e.g., plan-do-check-act)?

<--- Score

4. Does a troubleshooting guide exist or is it needed?

<--- Score

5. Is there documentation that will support the successful operation of the improvement?

<--- Score

6. How likely is the current Change advisory board plan to come in on schedule or on budget?

<--- Score

7. What can you control?

<--- Score

8. How does your workforce performance management system support high-performance work and workforce engagement; consider workforce compensation, reward, recognition, and incentive practices; and reinforce a customer and business focus and achievement of your action plans?

<--- Score

9. Who is the Change advisory board process owner?

<--- Score

10. Who will be in control?

<--- Score

11. What quality tools were useful in the control phase?

<--- Score

12. In the case of a Change advisory board project, the criteria for the audit derive from implementation objectives. an audit of a Change advisory board project involves assessing whether the recommendations outlined for implementation have been met. in other words, can we track that any Change advisory board project is implemented as planned, and is it working?
<--- Score

13. Are pertinent alerts monitored, analyzed and distributed to appropriate personnel?
<--- Score

14. Whats the best design framework for Change advisory board organization now that, in a post industrial-age if the top-down, command and control model is no longer relevant?
<--- Score

15. How will the process owner verify improvement in present and future sigma levels, process capabilities?
<--- Score

16. How will report readings be checked to effectively monitor performance?
<--- Score

17. How will input, process, and output variables be checked to detect for sub-optimal conditions?
<--- Score

18. Have new or revised work instructions resulted?
<--- Score

19. Is reporting being used or needed?
<--- Score

20. How might the organization capture best practices and lessons learned so as to leverage improvements across the business?
<--- Score

21. Is a response plan in place for when the input, process, or output measures indicate an 'out-of-control' condition?
<--- Score

22. What other areas of the organization might benefit from the Change advisory board team's improvements, knowledge, and learning?
<--- Score

23. Who controls critical resources?
<--- Score

24. Is knowledge gained on process shared and institutionalized?
<--- Score

25. Do the decisions we make today help people and the planet tomorrow?
<--- Score

26. What is our theory of human motivation, and how does our compensation plan fit with that view?
<--- Score

27. Do the Change advisory board decisions we

make today help people and the planet tomorrow?
<--- Score

28. Is there a control plan in place for sustaining improvements (short and long-term)?
<--- Score

29. What are the known security controls?
<--- Score

30. What are we attempting to measure/monitor?
<--- Score

31. What is your theory of human motivation, and how does your compensation plan fit with that view?
<--- Score

32. Are documented procedures clear and easy to follow for the operators?
<--- Score

33. Were the planned controls in place?
<--- Score

34. What should we measure to verify efficiency gains?
<--- Score

35. How will new or emerging customer needs/requirements be checked/communicated to orient the process toward meeting the new specifications and continually reducing variation?
<--- Score

36. Do you monitor the effectiveness of your Change advisory board activities?

<--- Score

37. What are the critical parameters to watch?
<--- Score

38. Is there a recommended audit plan for routine surveillance inspections of Change advisory board's gains?
<--- Score

39. What are your results for key measures or indicators of the accomplishment of your Change advisory board strategy and action plans, including building and strengthening core competencies?
<--- Score

40. How do our controls stack up?
<--- Score

41. What should the next improvement project be that is related to Change advisory board?
<--- Score

42. Does job training on the documented procedures need to be part of the process team's education and training?
<--- Score

43. How will the day-to-day responsibilities for monitoring and continual improvement be transferred from the improvement team to the process owner?
<--- Score

44. What are the key elements of your Change

advisory board performance improvement system, including your evaluation, organizational learning, and innovation processes?
<--- Score

45. Has the improved process and its steps been standardized?
<--- Score

46. Does the Change advisory board performance meet the customer's requirements?
<--- Score

47. Are new process steps, standards, and documentation ingrained into normal operations?
<--- Score

48. Are suggested corrective/restorative actions indicated on the response plan for known causes to problems that might surface?
<--- Score

49. Are controls in place and consistently applied?
<--- Score

50. Do we monitor the Change advisory board decisions made and fine tune them as they evolve?
<--- Score

51. Is a response plan established and deployed?
<--- Score

52. Were the planned controls working?
<--- Score

53. If there currently is no plan, will a plan be

developed?
<--- Score

54. Does Change advisory board appropriately measure and monitor risk?
<--- Score

55. Against what alternative is success being measured?
<--- Score

56. Who has control over resources?
<--- Score

57. Is there a standardized process?
<--- Score

58. Are operating procedures consistent?
<--- Score

59. Is there a Change advisory board Communication plan covering who needs to get what information when?
<--- Score

60. Is new knowledge gained imbedded in the response plan?
<--- Score

61. Why is change control necessary?
<--- Score

62. Will existing staff require re-training, for example, to learn new business processes?
<--- Score

63. What is the recommended frequency of auditing?
<--- Score

64. What key inputs and outputs are being measured on an ongoing basis?
<--- Score

65. How do we enable market innovation while controlling security and privacy?
<--- Score

66. What other systems, operations, processes, and infrastructures (hiring practices, staffing, training, incentives/rewards, metrics/dashboards/scorecards, etc.) need updates, additions, changes, or deletions in order to facilitate knowledge transfer and improvements?
<--- Score

67. Are there documented procedures?
<--- Score

68. What do we stand for--and what are we against?
<--- Score

69. What is your quality control system?
<--- Score

70. What is the control/monitoring plan?
<--- Score

71. Implementation Planning- is a pilot needed to test the changes before a full roll out occurs?
<--- Score

72. Will any special training be provided for results interpretation?
<--- Score

73. What should we measure to verify effectiveness gains?
<--- Score

74. Is there a transfer of ownership and knowledge to process owner and process team tasked with the responsibilities.
<--- Score

75. Is there a documented and implemented monitoring plan?
<--- Score

76. How will the process owner and team be able to hold the gains?
<--- Score

77. How can we best use all of our knowledge repositories to enhance learning and sharing?
<--- Score

78. How do you encourage people to take control and responsibility?
<--- Score

Add up total points for this section:
_ _ _ _ _ = Total points for this section

Divided by: _ _ _ _ _ _ (number of statements answered) = _ _ _ _ _ _
Average score for this section

Transfer your score to the Change
advisory board Index at the beginning
of the Self-Assessment.

CRITERION #7: SUSTAIN:

INTENT: Retain the benefits.

In my belief, the answer to this question is clearly defined:

5 Strongly Agree

4 Agree

3 Neutral

2 Disagree

1 Strongly Disagree

1. How can we incorporate support to ensure safe and effective use of Change advisory board into the services that we provide?
<--- Score

2. Who will be responsible for deciding whether Change advisory board goes ahead or not after the initial investigations?
<--- Score

3. What is our competitive advantage?

<--- Score

4. What are specific Change advisory board Rules to follow?
<--- Score

5. Do your leaders set clear a direction that is aligned with the vision, mission, and values and is cascaded throughout the organization with measurable goals?
<--- Score

6. What happens at this company when people fail?
<--- Score

7. Why should people listen to you?
<--- Score

8. If our customer were my grandmother, would I tell her to buy what we're selling?
<--- Score

9. Is maximizing Change advisory board protection the same as minimizing Change advisory board loss?
<--- Score

10. Would you rather sell to knowledgeable and informed customers or to uninformed customers?
<--- Score

11. What is the mission of the organization?
<--- Score

12. What counts that we are not counting?
<--- Score

13. What information is critical to our organization that our executives are ignoring?
<--- Score

14. Who will use it?
<--- Score

15. Do I know what I'm doing? And who do I call if I don't?
<--- Score

16. Are we changing as fast as the world around us?
<--- Score

17. What are your organizations work systems?
<--- Score

18. What are the short and long-term Change advisory board goals?
<--- Score

19. Who is going to care?
<--- Score

20. Is Change advisory board dependent on the successful delivery of a current project?
<--- Score

21. How do we make it meaningful in connecting Change advisory board with what users do day-to-day?
<--- Score

22. Do you keep 50% of your time unscheduled?
<--- Score

23. What are the business goals Change advisory board is aiming to achieve?
<--- Score

24. What was the last experiment we ran?
<--- Score

25. What stupid rule would we most like to kill?
<--- Score

26. What does your signature ensure?
<--- Score

27. If there were zero limitations, what would we do differently?
<--- Score

28. Why are Change advisory board skills important?
<--- Score

29. How do we provide a safe environment -physically and emotionally?
<--- Score

30. Did my employees make progress today?
<--- Score

31. If no one would ever find out about my accomplishments, how would I lead differently?
<--- Score

32. Ask yourself: how would we do this work if we only had one staff member to do it?
<--- Score

33. Do we say no to customers for no reason?
<--- Score

34. What am I trying to prove to myself, and how might it be hijacking my life and business success?
<--- Score

35. Who will provide the final approval of Change advisory board deliverables?
<--- Score

36. Who is responsible for errors?
<--- Score

37. How can you negotiate Change advisory board successfully with a stubborn boss, an irate client, or a deceitful coworker?
<--- Score

38. In what ways are Change advisory board vendors and us interacting to ensure safe and effective use?
<--- Score

39. What is our Change advisory board Strategy?
<--- Score

40. Who sets the Change advisory board standards?
<--- Score

41. Who will manage the integration of tools?
<--- Score

42. Are new benefits received and understood?
<--- Score

43. Will I get fired?

<--- Score

44. Schedule -can it be done in the given time?

<--- Score

45. Do you have an implicit bias for capital investments over people investments?

<--- Score

46. What happens if you do not have enough funding?

<--- Score

47. What will be the consequences to the stakeholder (financial, reputation etc) if Change advisory board does not go ahead or fails to deliver the objectives?

<--- Score

48. Is there any existing Change advisory board governance structure?

<--- Score

49. Who are four people whose careers I've enhanced?

<--- Score

50. How are we doing compared to our industry?

<--- Score

51. Where is your organization on the performance excellence continuum?

<--- Score

52. How do we manage Change advisory board Knowledge Management (KM)?

<--- Score

53. Do we have enough freaky customers in our portfolio pushing us to the limit day in and day out?
<--- Score

54. Political -is anyone trying to undermine this project?
<--- Score

55. Who are the key stakeholders?
<--- Score

56. Have benefits been optimized with all key stakeholders?
<--- Score

57. Have highly satisfied employees?
<--- Score

58. What will drive Change advisory board change?
<--- Score

59. How are conflicts dealt with?
<--- Score

60. What have we done to protect our business from competitive encroachment?
<--- Score

61. Are we relevant? Will we be relevant five years from now? Ten?
<--- Score

62. Who is the main stakeholder, with ultimate

responsibility for driving Change advisory board forward?
<--- Score

63. What new services of functionality will be implemented next with Change advisory board ?
<--- Score

64. What is the funding source for this project?
<--- Score

65. How to Secure Change advisory board?
<--- Score

66. What is something you believe that nearly no one agrees with you on?
<--- Score

67. What kind of crime could a potential new hire have committed that would not only not disqualify him/her from being hired by our organization, but would actually indicate that he/she might be a particularly good fit?
<--- Score

68. What are the long-term Change advisory board goals?
<--- Score

69. How is business? Why?
<--- Score

70. Has implementation been effective in reaching specified objectives?
<--- Score

71. If you were responsible for initiating and implementing major changes in your organization, what steps might you take to ensure acceptance of those changes?
<--- Score

72. How will you know that the Change advisory board project has been successful?
<--- Score

73. Have totally satisfied customers?
<--- Score

74. If our company went out of business tomorrow, would anyone who doesn't get a paycheck here care?
<--- Score

75. If we do not follow, then how to lead?
<--- Score

76. What knowledge, skills and characteristics mark a good Change advisory board project manager?
<--- Score

77. Who have we, as a company, historically been when we've been at our best?
<--- Score

78. Do you have a vision statement?
<--- Score

79. How do we foster innovation?
<--- Score

80. If we weren't already in this business, would we

enter it today? And if not, what are we going to do about it?

<--- Score

81. What would have to be true for the option on the table to be the best possible choice?

<--- Score

82. Is there any reason to believe the opposite of my current belief?

<--- Score

83. Do we have the right capabilities and capacities?

<--- Score

84. How do we engage the workforce, in addition to satisfying them?

<--- Score

85. How will we ensure we get what we expected?

<--- Score

86. How do we Lead with Change advisory board in Mind?

<--- Score

87. Who are you going to put out of business, and why?

<--- Score

88. What is Tricky About This?

<--- Score

89. Among our stronger employees, how many see themselves at the company in three years? How

many would leave for a 10 percent raise from another company?

<--- Score

90. Who uses our product in ways we never expected?

<--- Score

91. What are our long-range and short-range goals?

<--- Score

92. Who are our customers?

<--- Score

93. What may be the consequences for the performance of an organization if all stakeholders are not consulted regarding Change advisory board?

<--- Score

94. How do I stay inspired?

<--- Score

95. In retrospect, of the projects that we pulled the plug on, what percent do we wish had been allowed to keep going, and what percent do we wish had ended earlier?

<--- Score

96. Is our strategy driving our strategy? Or is the way in which we allocate resources driving our strategy?

<--- Score

97. Is a Change advisory board Team Work effort in place?

<--- Score

98. What do we do when new problems arise?
<--- Score

99. Whose voice (department, ethnic group, women, older workers, etc) might you have missed hearing from in your company, and how might you amplify this voice to create positive momentum for your business?
<--- Score

100. What potential megatrends could make our business model obsolete?
<--- Score

101. How do we keep the momentum going?
<--- Score

102. What role does communication play in the success or failure of a Change advisory board project?
<--- Score

103. Where is our petri dish?
<--- Score

104. How long will it take to change?
<--- Score

105. What is our mission?
<--- Score

106. How much does Change advisory board help?
<--- Score

107. What are your most important goals for the

strategic Change advisory board objectives?
<--- Score

108. What sources do you use to gather information for a Change advisory board study?
<--- Score

109. Has the investment re-baselined during the past fiscal year?
<--- Score

110. What business benefits will Change advisory board goals deliver if achieved?
<--- Score

111. How will we know when our strategy has been successful?
<--- Score

112. Do we underestimate the customer's journey?
<--- Score

113. Who, on the executive team or the board, has spoken to a customer recently?
<--- Score

114. What are the usability implications of Change advisory board actions?
<--- Score

115. What is Effective Change advisory board?
<--- Score

116. What principles do we value?
<--- Score

117. How do you listen to customers to obtain actionable information?

<--- Score

118. Which models, tools and techniques are necessary?

<--- Score

119. What threat is Change advisory board addressing?

<--- Score

120. Have new benefits been realized?

<--- Score

121. What are the success criteria that will indicate that Change advisory board objectives have been met and the benefits delivered?

<--- Score

122. To whom do you add value?

<--- Score

123. What one word do we want to own in the minds of our customers, employees, and partners?

<--- Score

124. What is performance excellence?

<--- Score

125. Legal and contractual - are we allowed to do this?

<--- Score

126. What external factors influence our success?

<--- Score

127. What is our formula for success in Change advisory board ?

<--- Score

128. When information truly is ubiquitous, when reach and connectivity are completely global, when computing resources are infinite, and when a whole new set of impossibilities are not only possible, but happening, what will that do to our business?

<--- Score

129. Who is responsible for ensuring appropriate resources (time, people and money) are allocated to Change advisory board?

<--- Score

130. What are strategies for increasing support and reducing opposition?

<--- Score

131. What is the purpose of Change advisory board in relation to the mission?

<--- Score

132. Is the impact that Change advisory board has shown?

<--- Score

133. Are we paying enough attention to the partners our company depends on to succeed?

<--- Score

134. Are there Change advisory board Models?

<--- Score

135. Who do we want our customers to become?
<--- Score

136. The Change advisory board is defined
<--- Score

137. What is the craziest thing we can do?
<--- Score

138. Were lessons learned captured and communicated?
<--- Score

139. What is it like to work for me?
<--- Score

140. How will we insure seamless interoperability of Change advisory board moving forward?
<--- Score

141. What is a feasible sequencing of reform initiatives over time?
<--- Score

142. If I had to leave my organization for a year and the only communication I could have with employees was a single paragraph, what would I write?
<--- Score

143. Think about the kind of project structure that would be appropriate for your Change advisory board project. should it be formal and complex, or can it be less formal and relatively simple?
<--- Score

144. If we got kicked out and the board brought in a

new CEO, what would he do?
<--- Score

145. Who Uses What?
<--- Score

146. Operational - will it work?
<--- Score

147. How would our PR, marketing, and social media change if we did not use outside agencies?
<--- Score

148. What are your key business, operational, societal responsibility, and human resource strategic challenges and advantages?
<--- Score

149. What is our question?
<--- Score

150. What happens when a new employee joins the organization?
<--- Score

151. The Change Advisory Board role is defined
<--- Score

152. Will it be accepted by users?
<--- Score

153. What are the critical success factors?
<--- Score

154. How do we maintain Change advisory board's Integrity?

<--- Score

155. Which Change advisory board goals are the most important?

<--- Score

156. Who will determine interim and final deadlines?

<--- Score

157. Which criteria are used to determine which projects are going to be pursued or discarded?

<--- Score

158. You may have created your customer policies at a time when you lacked resources, technology wasn't up-to-snuff, or low service levels were the industry norm. Have those circumstances changed?

<--- Score

159. What current systems have to be understood and/or changed?

<--- Score

160. Am I failing differently each time?

<--- Score

161. Why don't our customers like us?

<--- Score

162. Are we making progress? and are we making progress as Change advisory board leaders?

<--- Score

163. Do we have the right people on the bus?

<--- Score

164. Will there be any necessary staff changes (redundancies or new hires)?
<--- Score

165. Are there any disadvantages to implementing Change advisory board? There might be some that are less obvious?
<--- Score

166. What is a good product?
<--- Score

167. How will we know if we have been successful?
<--- Score

168. Are we making progress?
<--- Score

169. Is the Change advisory board organization completing tasks effectively and efficiently?
<--- Score

170. How important is Change advisory board to the user organizations mission?
<--- Score

171. Which individuals, teams or departments will be involved in Change advisory board?
<--- Score

172. Are you satisfied with your current role? If not, what is missing from it?
<--- Score

173. What is an unauthorized commitment?
<--- Score

174. How do senior leaders deploy your organizations vision and values through your leadership system, to the workforce, to key suppliers and partners, and to customers and other stakeholders, as appropriate?
<--- Score

175. If you had to rebuild your organization without any traditional competitive advantages (i.e., no killer a technology, promising research, innovative product/service delivery model, etc.), how would your people have to approach their work and collaborate together in order to create the necessary conditions for success?
<--- Score

176. Do you have any supplemental information to add to this checklist?
<--- Score

177. Is it economical; do we have the time and money?
<--- Score

178. What are the Essentials of Internal Change advisory board Management?
<--- Score

179. What trouble can we get into?
<--- Score

180. We picked a method, now what?
<--- Score

181. How likely is it that a customer would recommend our company to a friend or colleague?
<--- Score

182. Are the criteria for selecting recommendations stated?

<--- Score

183. What would I recommend my friend do if he were facing this dilemma?
<--- Score

184. What are the rules and assumptions my industry operates under? What if the opposite were true?
<--- Score

185. How do you determine the key elements that affect Change advisory board workforce satisfaction? how are these elements determined for different workforce groups and segments?

<--- Score

186. What did we miss in the interview for the worst hire we ever made?
<--- Score

187. What are the gaps in my knowledge and experience?
<--- Score

188. In a project to restructure Change advisory board outcomes, which stakeholders would you involve?

<--- Score

189. Who is On the Team?

<--- Score

190. Do we think we know, or do we know we know ?

<--- Score

191. How Do We Know if We Are Successful?

<--- Score

192. What is the estimated value of the project?

<--- Score

193. How do we ensure that implementations of Change advisory board products are done in a way that ensures safety?

<--- Score

194. How do we go about Securing Change advisory board?

<--- Score

195. How do we accomplish our long range Change advisory board goals?

<--- Score

196. Instead of going to current contacts for new ideas, what if you reconnected with dormant contacts--the people you used to know? If you were going reactivate a dormant tie, who would it be?

<--- Score

197. Marketing budgets are tighter, consumers are more skeptical, and social media has changed forever the way we talk about Change advisory board. How do we gain traction?

<--- Score

198. But does it really, really work?
<--- Score

199. How do we foster the skills, knowledge, talents, attributes, and characteristics we want to have?
<--- Score

200. How much contingency will be available in the budget?
<--- Score

201. How to deal with Change advisory board Changes?
<--- Score

202. Is there a lack of internal resources to do this work?
<--- Score

203. How can we become the company that would put us out of business?
<--- Score

204. How do senior leaders set organizational vision and values?
<--- Score

205. Who else should we help?
<--- Score

206. In the past year, what have you done (or could you have done) to increase the accurate perception of this company/brand as ethical and honest?

<--- Score

207. How does Change advisory board integrate with other business initiatives?
<--- Score

208. Are we making progress (as leaders)?
<--- Score

209. Are we / should we be Revolutionary or evolutionary?
<--- Score

210. Think of your Change advisory board project. what are the main functions?
<--- Score

211. What are internal and external Change advisory board relations?
<--- Score

212. Do Change advisory board rules make a reasonable demand on a users capabilities?
<--- Score

213. Why should we adopt a Change advisory board framework?
<--- Score

214. What is the overall business strategy?
<--- Score

215. Do you see more potential in people than they do in themselves?
<--- Score

216. Are assumptions made in Change advisory board stated explicitly?

<--- Score

217. Whom among your colleagues do you trust, and for what?

<--- Score

218. Are the assumptions believable and achievable?

<--- Score

219. What are the challenges?

<--- Score

220. How will we build a 100-year startup?

<--- Score

221. Which functions and people interact with the supplier and or customer?

<--- Score

222. Where can we break convention?

<--- Score

223. What should we stop doing?

<--- Score

224. Can we maintain our growth without detracting from the factors that have contributed to our success?

<--- Score

225. How do you govern and fulfill your societal responsibilities?

<--- Score

226. What are we challenging, in the sense that Mac challenged the PC or Dove tackled the Beauty Myth?
<--- Score

227. Who do we think the world wants us to be?
<--- Score

228. How can we become more high-tech but still be high touch?
<--- Score

229. What trophy do we want on our mantle?
<--- Score

230. What are all of our Change advisory board domains and what do they do?
<--- Score

231. What is your BATNA (best alternative to a negotiated agreement)?
<--- Score

232. How Do We Create Buy-in?
<--- Score

233. What is the range of capabilities?
<--- Score

234. What management system can we use to leverage the Change advisory board experience, ideas, and concerns of the people closest to the work to be done?
<--- Score

Add up total points for this section:

_____ = Total points for this section

Divided by: _____ (number of
statements answered) = _____
Average score for this section

Transfer your score to the Change
advisory board Index at the beginning
of the Self-Assessment.

Index

Lightning Source UK Ltd.
Milton Keynes UK
UKHW020637170719
346320UK00013B/618/P

9 780655 194804